PASSPORT
UNITED
KINGDOM

D1738743

Passport to the World

Passport Argentina
Passport Brazil
Passport China
Passport France
Passport Germany
Passport Hong Kong
Passport India
Passport Israel
Passport Italy
Passport Japan
Passport Korea
Passport Malaysia
Passport Mexico
Passport Philippines
Passport Russia
Passport Singapore
Passport South Africa
Passport Spain
Passport Taiwan
Passport Thailand
Passport USA
Passport Vietnam

PASSPORT
UNITED
KINGDOM

Your Pocket Guide
to
British Business,
Customs & Etiquette

Timothy Harper

Passport Series Editor: Barbara Szerlip

WORLD TRADE PRESS®
Professional Books for International Trade

World Trade Press
1505 Fifth Avenue
San Rafael, California 94901 USA
Tel: (415) 454-9934
Fax: (415) 453-7980
USA Order Line: (800) 833-8586
E-mail: WorldPress@aol.com

"Passport to the World" concept: Edward Hinkelman
Cover and book design: Peter Jones
Illustrations: Tom Watson

Library of Congress Cataloging-in-Publication Data
Harper, Timothy, 1950–
Passport United Kingdom: your pocket guide to British business, customs & etiquette / Tim Harper.
p. cm. -- (Passport to the world)
ISBN 1-885073-28-3
1. Corporate culture -- Great Britain. 2. Business etiquette -- Great Britain.
3. Industrial management -- Social aspects -- Great Britain. 4. Intercul-
tural communication. I. Title. II. Series.
HD58.7.H36925 1996
390'.00941 -- dc20
96-28182
CIP

Printed in the United States of America

Table of Contents
United Kingdom

England, N. Ireland, Scotland & Wales

 Doing Business Across Cultures

Internationally Speaking

The past decade has seen a dramatic lowering of trade barriers, the globalization of markets, and explosive growth in international trade. As a result, the business world has become increasingly interdependent, creating both new challenges and exciting new opportunities.

In order to conduct business abroad, you need to understand the environments in which your foreign counterparts operate. You will probably never know a particular culture as well as your own — not only is the language different, but the historical and cultural context within which its people operate is often misunderstood by outsiders.

Think Globally, Act Locally

Although business operations around the world have become highly internationalized, national traditions, attitudes and beliefs remain diverse. Everyone's perceptions — what we see, hear, taste, touch and smell — are filtered through a particular set of habits and assumptions. When you understand that your own cultural background colors your world view, you can begin to appreciate that your foreign associate may have an entirely different perspective, and that he or she may approach a situation in a totally different and unexpected way.

For example, whereas Westerners tend to value individuality of thought and action, Eastern cultures prize conformity and harmony of purpose. While an Englishman's primary focus may be to conclude the business at hand, a Mexican will concentrate on first developing a personal relationship. Public praise is much enjoyed by North Americans, but it is a source of embarrassment and discomfort for the Japanese.

Passport United Kingdom

Gaining a thorough understanding of a people can take several years of living and working among them — and sometimes not even that is sufficient. However, you can increase your chances of achieving harmonious and profitable relationships by learning something about your associate's point of view and adjusting your behavior accordingly.

Passport United Kingdom will introduce you to the United Kingdom's business culture and offer insights into how the local traditions, etiquette, values and communication styles differ from your own.

Comparing Values Across Cultures	
One Culture:	**Another Culture:**
Values change	Values tradition
Favors specific communication	Favors ambiguous communication
Values analytical, linear problem solving	Values intuitive, lateral problem solving
Places emphasis on individual performance	Places emphasis on group performance
Considers verbal communication most important	Considers context & nonverbal communication most important
Focuses on task and product	Focuses on relationship and process
Places emphasis on promoting differing views	Places emphasis on harmony and consensus
Emphasizes competition	Emphasizes collaboration
Prefers informal tone	Prefers formal tone
Is flexible about schedules	Emphasizes rigid adherence to schedules

United Kingdom
Quick Look

Official name	United Kingdom of Great Britain and Northern Ireland
Total area	244,820 sq km
Capital & largest city	London (6.9 million)

People

Population (1995)	58,295,119
Density	238 per sq mile
Annual growth	0.27%
Distribution	(in millions)

England 48
Scotland 5
Wales 3
N. Ireland 2

Languages	English, Welsh, Gaelic
Major religions	Church of England, Roman Catholic, Presbyterian

Economy (1994)

GDP	US$1 trillion
	US$18,000 per capita
Foreign trade (1994)	Imports — US$215 billion
	Exports — US$200 billion
Principal trade partners	Germany
	USA
	France
	Netherlands
Currency	Pound Sterling (£)
	£1 = 100 pence
Exchange Rate (7/96)	£1 = US$1.5525

Education and health

Literacy (1995 est)	99%
Universities (1991 est)	43 (Gr. Britain), 2 (N. Ireland)
Life expectancy (1995)	Women................80.0 years
	Men......................74.2 years
Infant mortality (1995)	7 deaths per 1,000 live births

UNITED KINGDOM

2 Country Facts

Geography

The United Kingdom of Great Britain and Northern Ireland was established in 1801 and covers an area about the size of the U.S. state of Oregon. It's separated from the coast of western Europe by the English Channel to the south and the North Sea to the east. The northern and western shores are bounded by the Atlantic. The terrain ranges from rugged hills and low mountains to rolling plains. Because of its heavily indented coastline, no place is more than 75 miles from the sea.

The terms England, Britain and United Kingdom can be hard to differentiate. Great Britain is comprised of England, Scotland and Wales, along with the Isle of Man and the Channel Islands (notably Jersey, Guernsey, Alderney and Sark). When Northern Ireland is added, it becomes the United Kingdom.

Britain's political divisions are reflected in its national flag, the Union Jack — the red cross of Saint George (England), the white saltire of Saint Andrew (Scotland) and Ireland's red saltire, all dislayed on a blue background. Wales is a principality, a country without a government.

Scotland retains a few remnants of its national independence, including aspects of home rule that allow self-determination for certain local laws and regulations (such as shopping hours and pub closing times). Both Scotland and Wales have small independence movements, but independence from the United Kingdom is unlikely in the near or distant future. Nonetheless, it is politically incorrect, if not impolite, to refer to Wales as part of England or to lump the Scots in with the English.

The province of Northern Ireland is the result of the partition of Ireland early in the 20th century. Britain insisted on maintaining political control of Ireland's northern counties in order to protect the majority of the population, who viewed themselves as British rather than Irish.

Demographics

WASPs (white Anglo-Saxon Protestants) still make up the largest segment of the U.K.'s population, but their traditional majority status has been undermined in recent years by immigration. The largest minorities hail from former British colonies — notably such now-independent countries on the Asian subcontinent as India and Pakistan, as well as Caribbean nations and protectorates. Many British blacks prefer to be known as Afro-Caribbeans.

England's population is concentrated in the southeast, around London and the surrounding Home Counties, notably County Kent — a rich "breadbasket" that has also benefited from the development of two of Europe's largest shopping centers and construction of the Channel Tunnel that links England and France.

Climate

Britain is a damp, foggy, temperate island in the North Sea. Its weather rarely dips below freezing (that's why the water pipes are on the outside of so many houses) or rises above 80° Fahrenheit. In recent years, however, the extremes have become somewhat more extreme, and there have been a number of warm ("beastly hot," the Brits used to say) summers, with daylight sometimes lasting past 10 P.M. Still, anything above 75° is considered a heat wave, and even those temperatures can seem unpleasant to people living and working in buildings where air conditioning remains a luxury. Winter brings snow (except in London and the South) and as little as six hours of flinty daylight, with the chill borne by breezes off the sea cutting to the bone.

Business Hours

Most stores and shops open by 9 or 9:30 A.M. Offices *button up* by 5 or 6 P.M. with many government offices closing earlier. Large department stores and supermarkets stay open until 9 P.M. or later. Pubs generally operate between 11 A.M. and 11 P.M., with a break between 3 and 5:30. In many commercial and tourist areas, however, pubs stay open all afternoon and sometimes later on the weekends.

National (Bank) Holidays

The following are days when most businesses are closed:

New Year's Day ....January 1

Good Friday ....(March or April)
    The anniversary of Jesus Christ's crucifiction.

Easter Monday ....(March or April)
    Commemoration of Christ's resurrection.

Early May Bank Holiday ....the first Monday in
                                         May

Late May Bank Holiday ....the last Monday in
                                         May

Late Summer Bank Holiday ....the last Monday in
                                         August

Christmas Day...........................December 25
    Celebration of Christ's birth.

Boxing Day ....December 26
    Boxed holiday gifts are given to mailmen, housekeepers and other service workers.

Professionals and managers usually enjoy two to four weeks of vacation in July or August.

Informal Holidays

The Queen's Birthday (celebrated the second Saturday in June) features a parade in London and plenty of horses and regalia.

Remembrance Day (the Sunday closest to November 11th) commemorates the end of war hostilities in 1918 and 1945.

Mothering Sunday honors mothers (early spring).

For more on holidays, see Customs (Chapter 17).

 ## The British

Language

Britain's language, like its royalty, is Germanic in origin — though the language seems to be faring better in recent years, at least in terms of popularity and influence, than the House of Windsor. English was also influenced by Celtic, Norse, Anglo-Saxon, Latin and Norman French, the language spoken by the Nordic tribes that took over northern France in the Dark Ages and then England in the 11th century.

Today, English has become the international language of business, science and technology, and the British think that's as it should be. Still, even native speakers from places like the United States, Canada and Australia can find British English challenging.

Sorry!

Sorry is probably the most used — and most misunderstood — word in British English. Among its many meanings: "Get out of the way," when uttered brusquely; "You idiot," when spoken sarcastically or impatiently; "Excuse me," when said meekly or contritely; "I don't understand" or "I didn't hear you" are also common meanings. Once in a great while, it actually can be an expression of regret. But not very often.

Origin of Famous Phrases

Around the Inns of Court, the heart of legal London, barristers in their black robes and short gray wigs can be seen cozying up to judges with longer hairpieces, the "big wigs." Clerks scurry to and fro carrying legal documents tied with pink ribbon — "red tape."

"Dressed to kill" refers to the 17th century gentlemen who donned their best silk attire before fighting duels. The expression "cock and bull story" derives from the outlandish stories drivers told passengers on the old carriage route to the Cock and Bull Pub.

"Pulling your leg" dates from the era of public hangings, when condemned men feared that death would be slow and painful. They would persuade a relative or friend, or sometimes pay someone, to yank their legs down to ensure that their necks broke quickly and cleanly.

The term "posh" is an acronym for the luxury class on sailing ships to India (the jewel in the crown of the old British Empire). The best cabins avoided the hot sun: Port Out, Starboard Home.

Accents: How You Speak Is Who You Are

The modern English accent is a relatively recent affectation, initially taken up by the upper classes in the 1700s and 1800s as a means of distinguishing themselves from the rabble. (Prior to that, the British supposedly sounded very much like today's North Americans.) Gradually, what began as a tool for snobbery was adopted by all levels of society (with the exception of various telling sub-accents). The upper class tends to change -*er* endings to -*ah*, as in "He's a big spend-*ah*," or to pronounce the name Lander as *Lan-dah*. Don't assume that you know how to spell someone's name based on its pronunciation.

Until recently, an uppercrust London-centered accent — the accent of radio and television news announcers (a.k.a. *Standard English* or *BBC-Speak*) — was thought to reflect a proper upbringing and a university education. It was in a Briton's best interest to learn it before entering the business world, even if he or she had grown up speaking with a clipped Scottish dialect, the flat, nasal tones of northern England, the guttural broad accent of the West County or any of the many other linguistic identifiers. But today, regional accents have become quite acceptable and in some professions (media, marketing, entertainment) are very trendy.

Rhyming Slang

Accents become more impenetrable the farther you get from big-city business and entertainment centers. Even in London, however, the Cockney (or working class) accent is often befuddling. Motor (another word for automobile) is pronounced *Mo-ah* and Peter is *Pee-ah*. *Oy* is the Cockney way of saying "Hey," often in a way designed to show irritation. To complicate matters, Cockneys — technically, people born within the sound of the bells of St. Mary le Bow Church in London's East End — rely on a traditional rhyming slang: *Trouble and Strife* means wife, for example; *Cash and Carried* is married, *Kidney Punch* is lunch, *Dog and Bone* is the telephone, and so on.

The ethnic dialects of Britons with an Indian subcontinent or Afro-Caribbean heritage can also be difficult for the uninitiated, as can the accents of the working class in Glasgow, Manchester and Cardiff. Sometimes the only way a foreigner can hold a conversation is with regular interruptions to ask for repeats or clarifications. Be sure to say *sorry* like you really mean it.

The Family

Many Britons spend an inordinate amount of time, most notably at Christmas, with parents, grandparents, children, cousins and in-laws they don't particularly like. It's a tradition, and the British are nothing if not traditional.

Like so much else in British life, childhood is seen as something to be "gotten through"(see *stiff upper lip*, page 23). Among the upper classes, hired nannies and governesses, rather than parents, do the actual child-rearing, and in some families, the children are routinely shipped off to boarding school (to learn self-sufficiency and other character-building skills) before the age of ten.

Class: A Dying Concept?

Society is gradually becoming more fluid, even in steadfast England. But many working-class families still believe that their children are destined to live out their lives as working-class adults. And many upper-class parents are convinced they're handing down the birthright of privilege.

While in some countries a vast majority of the population would describe themselves as middle class, the term in Britain carries a meaning closer to bourgeois or upper middle class. Britain's middle class is typified by the striving professional or manager who earned his or her position by way of education and merit, and who earns well above typical wages.

There is an uneasy sense that society has become more aggressive, more transitional, more transactional — more "American," in other words. But at certain times, there is also a strong sense that tradition matters and can be counted on, such as when Parliament officially opens, or when the Queen presents her annual Christmas address. (She rarely says anything interesting, but the whole country stops for 10 minutes to look and listen.) Tradition means continuity, and continuity means that the past will always have its place.

How the British View Themselves

If they weren't superior, how is it that their foggy little island nation could have played such a major role in world history? How is it that their language has become so important throughout the world? The British see their culture — from Shakespeare and Isaac Newton to Winston Churchill and the Beatles — as tremendously influential. Other British contributions to world culture include the concept of free, mandatory public education, the principles of common law and the parliamentary system (seminal to modern democracy). The first man to successfully scale Mount Everest was a Briton. The U.K. was the birthplace of Charles Darwin, Elizabeth I, Henry VIII, Bertrand Russell, G. B. Shaw, Oscar Wilde, W.B. Yeats, Benjamin Disraeli, Jane Austen and *Winnie the Pooh* (not to mention Jack the Ripper).

They see themselves as simply the most civilized people on earth: well educated, well mannered, knowing their roles in life and how to carry them out. It's good to have money, but not to want money. It's permissible to be successful, but not to show how enjoyable success can be.

The British regard themselves as cool and detached, but willing to take whatever action is necessary. Think of novelist Ian Fleming's suave, imperturbable hero, James Bond, a.k.a. Agent 007. He could mix a perfect martini ("shaken, not stirred"), fend off gorgeous (but duplicitious) women and, in his spare time, save the world from diabolical terrorists — all without wrinkling his tuxedo (or as the British would say, *dinner jacket*).

As the rest of Europe becomes more unified, the British insist on seeing themselves as Europeans by an accident of geography only. They already know all they need to know. And the British Isles, they point out, aren't really connected to Europe anyway.

Attitudes Toward Other Cultures

The British tend to regard other countries (including the European ones) as disorganized and crass, or at best, cheap copies of British culture. They also tend to think that anyone who isn't British would like to be, and that many try — foreign businesspeople who adapt English accents overnight, foreign heiresses who spend enough on charity and social events to be introduced to the fringe royalty, or foreign scholars who hurl themselves into the academic traditions of Oxford or Cambridge. Alas, the British are convinced that being British is something that can only be born into. As a result, British wannabes are taken for all they are worth and laughed at behind their backs.

A crueler manifestation of the British attitude toward other cultures is racism (and, to a lesser extent, anti-semitism). There is, for example, an obvious discrepancy between the number of caucasians and the number of "people of color" who are called over for questioning at customs at Heathrow or Gatwick airports on any given day.

National Identity and Pride

In the 19th century, Great Britain was the strongest power in Europe (and the birthplace of the Industrial Revolution). Though things have changed considerably since the days when the empire was so vast that "the sun never set" on it — India, Egypt, various African colonies, Hong Kong, New Zealand, Australia and Canada were all among its territories — history remains a great source of national pride.

Today, the U.K. is one of the world's great trading powers, and its economy ranks among the four largest in Western Europe. Still, national identity is usually left to politicians figuratively wrapping themselves in the Union Jack to fend off regulation from the European Union, or to soccer hooligans who roam the streets terrorizing the fans of opposing teams. (Between 1985 and 1990, English soccer teams were banned from Europe for just that reason.) One of the most devastating blows to national pride — and it's been happening more and more frequently — is a defeat of the English national football (soccer) team by teams from countries with less of a background in this British sport (some Asian or African nation, for example, or, worst of all, Germany or the United States).

Cultural Stereotypes

While cultural perceptions about the British vary, some are universal.

Class Snobs

The British judge people by the class they were born into, not by their merits.

British politicians and newspapers have been declaring for decades that the class system is dead, but most Britons still view themselves — and, more importantly, every other Briton — as either working class, middle class or upper class. The working class is vast, while the middle class is a relatively small bourgeoisie of mostly high-earning, university-educated, professional manager types.

It's becoming increasingly possible for someone born into a working-class family to rise to the middle class. But it's difficult for anyone not born into the upper class — landed gentry with estates, inheritances, titles and invitations to all the correct society parties — to ever enter it. Today's celebrities and entrepreneurs often work and play with the upper class but (as far as the latter are concerned) will never be "to the manor born."

Uptight

The British are perennially poker-faced, incapable of expressing honest emotion, and they dislike change.

The British reputation for reserve is deserved. Public displays of emotion would be frowned upon, if frowning wasn't a display of emotion. For some, a timely clearing of the throat is akin to a screaming tantrum. The traditional *stiff upper lip* (the ability to confront adversity with courage and strength of character) seems to manifest itself literally, rather than figuratively, and this can be problematic for visitors looking for some indication of what a Briton is really thinking.

Be careful about asking the British too many personal questions too quickly. It makes them uncomfortable, in part because they're naturally reserved. And in part because even a seemingly innocent question such as "Where did you go to school?" is seen as invasive by a Briton who knows that the answer (at least to another Briton) will reveal much about his parentage, upbringing, education and social standing.

They are, generally speaking, proponents of "the tried and true," preferring routine and familiarity to innovation or impulse. Why "update" something that's worked perfectly well for generations, or even centuries? Prince Charles has been very vocal about wanting all of Britain's buildings to follow historical models. Princess Anne is said to be perfectly happy dining on smoked salmon every day of the year. When British Telecom decided to change the color of their public telephone booths, the outcry was deafening.

Mannered but Not Well-Mannered

The British have lovely table manners but lousy people skills.

All Britons know to always hold the fork in the left hand and to tip the bowl away when finishing the soup. For visitors from countries with strong service-oriented economies, however, it can be jarring to encounter receptionists and shop clerks who prefer to talk among themselves, or to friends on the telephone, while ignoring the customers standing in front of them.

Even when you do manage to get someone's attention, they will sometimes be rude. The most effective weapon is to ask what you have done to offend. The British hate confrontations, and they hate being accused of rudeness. Explain that you are a visitor and that if you behaved impolitely, it was out of ignorance and accident. Almost invariably, you will be treated better.

Inedible Food

The British survive on a diet of starches, fats and sweets, and they overcook everything.

Britain may have the worst reputation for food in the industrialized world. The French say that the British set the table beautifully, but have no idea what to serve on it.

Breakfast is the one exception — eggs, bacon, sausage, kippers (smoked herring fried in butter), finnan haddie (smoked haddock), grilled tomatoes, porridge, toast and marmalade. What the English call "pudding" may confuse the uninitiated: Yorkshire pudding is a baked batter served with meats, while black pudding is a blood sausage best reserved for the brave.

Things are changing, though, particularly in London, where one can find restaurants serving the ethnic foods of dozens of nations.

Pets, Not People

The British care more for animals than friends or family.

Stories abound of people leaving vast sums of money to their pet cats and dogs in their wills. It's been said that the Royal Society for the Prevention of Cruelty to Animals receives more public support than the Society for the Prevention of Cruelty to Children (and it's noteworthy that the former has royal endorsement, while the latter is merely national).

However, the stereotype that the British love their dogs more than their children isn't strictly true; many British people love their dogs more than they love anyone, not just their children.

Sexually Repressed

British males have a puerile attitude toward women and sex.

Despite examples in literature of the dashing Englishman, this stereotype persists. The British themselves tend to encourage it, through television programs like *Benny Hill* and *Monty Python's Flying Circus.*

The longtime penchant for cross-dressing, particularly among the upper classes, may not be as publicly prevalent as in the past, but it's still evident — particularly during the Christmas "pantomime" season, when celebrities appear in opposite-gender roles in fractured-fairytale productions that mix a bit of social and political satire with heavy doses of double entendre and sexual innuendo.

Despite being ruled by a queen for the past forty-plus years and having had a powerful woman prime minister (Margaret Thatcher in the 1980s), Britain remains a paternalistic society often dominated by an old boy network.

An Island of Eccentrics

A lot of British live strange, quirky lives.

In a society that puts a lot of emphasis on doing the right thing, it gives the British a sense of humanity to tolerate people who erect "follies" (huge monuments to nothing in the countryside, for instance), travel the world collecting different kinds of toilet seats, or squirrel themselves away for forty years trying to learn Sanskrit. Train spotters travel the countryside by rail, studying the most achingly minute details of locomotives — everything from cross-ties to upholstery weaves and dimpled side panel rivets.

One of Charles Dickens' more memorable characters is Miss Havisham, in the 19th century novel *Great Expectations*. Having been "stood up" at the altar, she spends the rest of her life as a recluse, dressed in her wedding gown, surrounded by the decaying wedding feast. In a real-life, 20th-century version, a young chemist by the name of Joan Abery, a jilted bride-to-be, built herself a nest in a tree behind her mother's house in Reading, which she decorated with broken umbrellas and other discarded objects. She lived in it for thirty-five years, until her death in 1992, at the age of seventy.

Every now and then, someone does a study about how "The Great English Eccentric" is alive and well, and everyone feels better knowing that at least someone can be openly different, even if they, themselves, cannot.

Regional Differences

Scots

Scots (never to be confused with Scotch, which is a whisky) view their ethnic origins as Celtic — about 60,000 of them speak a form of Gaelic. They dislike being confused with their neighboring Anglo-Saxons (whom they regard as aloof and dour). And they're fond of pointing out how London sportscasters refer to athletes from England as English and athletes from Scotland as British — unless they lose badly, in which case they become Scottish. While the Scots often joke about their reputation for being cheap (or *canny*, as they would say), they are, in fact, among the most generous people in the world. However, they're not above using that reputation to their advantage when negotiating with foreigners.

The Scots are famous for their tartans — woolen plaids (with names like Black Watch, Royal Stuart and Campbell) fashioned into kilts (pleated skirts traditionally worn by men) — which have served as emblems for the Highland Clans since the 17th century. Today, though they account for only 1.5 percent of Europe's population, Scots produce 36 percent of European-made personal computers.

Welsh

Just as Scots suffer, however cheerfully, with their reputation for being tight-fisted, the people of Wales have to live with the linguistic inequity of the term *welsh*, as in "not paying off a debt." Like the Scots, they have their own language, which is distinguished by having some of the longest words — replete with W for a vowel and lots of double L's — in the world. (About one-quarter of the population speaks it.) As a race, they are tough on the outside and sensitive on the inside, part rugged coal miner and part Dylan Thomas (who remains a national hero as much for his legendary drinking binges as for his lyrical poems). And like the Scots, they see their distance from London as a virtue. Tourists and foreign businesspeople are welcome, but English people who buy country cottages in the hope of spending weekends in quaint, "backward" Welsh settings are often resented.

Northern Irish

Many of the roughly 1 million Protestants of Northern Ireland, descendants of the Scots and English who emigrated to Ulster, think of themselves as British. Many of the roughly 500,000 Catholics, descendants of centuries of Irish people, prefer to call themselves Irish and to think of their province as the part of Ireland that's being held — occupied, some would say — by the British military.

For a quarter of a century, Northern Ireland has been the battleground of a civil war, known locally as "The Troubles." Bombings, kidnappings, shootings, interrogations, vigilantism and mass arrests have been a way of life. However, recent ceasefires, combined with some of the fastest economic growth in Europe, has increased the possibility of a permanent peace.

More than 80 international shipping lines operate out of Northern Ireland's four main ports, linking the country to almost every point on the globe.

London-centric

Many Londoners are quite happy to live their entire lives without ever visiting such historic and now-bustling cities as Birmingham, Manchester, Liverpool and Newcastle. Both natives and transplants tend to think of anyone who lives and works in the hinterlands (anywhere other than London) as suspicious and unsophisticated. Clearly, they must not have the ability or the wherewithal to succeed in the capital, which has been a center of world power (exemplified by magnificent kings and queens) for more than a thousand years.

Regional Sports

Rugby, when played in the South, is called Rugby Union, and many top-level players are amateurs who have daytime jobs. Played in the North, it becomes Rugby League, with mostly professional players and an entirely different set of rules aimed at making the game faster.

Cricket, with its upper-class, private-school cachet, is more popular in the South. (In common parlance, when something is *not cricket*, it means that something's wrong, that rules have been broken. It's the opposite of *keeping a straight bat*, or playing fairly.) Be forewarned: international matches can last for five or six days, with breaks for meals, rain, tea, injuries, rest and stray dogs, and they're often declared a draw in the end.

6 — Government & Business

After World War II, many sectors of the British economy were nationalized. But since the Conservative Party came to power in the early 1980s under Margaret Thatcher, the privatization of industry has been encouraged, social welfare spending has been reduced, and interest rates have been held down. John Major has continued these policies into the 1990s, and Britain now has one of the most pro-business governments in the world. London ranks with New York City as a leading international financial center.

Companies in the U.K. pay a 33 percent corporate tax on profits — one of the lowest rates in the E.U. And there are no exchange controls or restrictions on sending those profits abroad. Labor costs are relatively low, and the U.K.'s per capita expenditures on research and development are the third highest in Europe.

The government supports a range of national, regional and local commissions and agencies that provide information to companies considering doing business in the United Kingdom — including branches, partnerships and joint ventures. In some cases, these commissions and agencies can even help scout locations, set up training programs and arrange for various financial incentives (particularily for businesses that generate local employment).

Barriers to Trade and Competition

In the course of trying to create a single trading bloc within Europe, the European Union has established many restrictions on individuals and companies from non-E.U. countries. As a result, it's much easier for a Frenchman or an Italian, for example, to start doing business in Britain than it is for an American or a Japanese. In some cases, non-Europeans must first prove that they are bringing a large amount of working capital into the country. Work permits are another obstacle; a non-European employee or employer may be required to submit extensive paperwork proving that the job cannot be filled by a British person before a work permit is granted.

Politics & Business

The economic growth of Britain and the public popularity of the Thatcher-Major business stance has led the main opposition group, the Labor Party, to move away from its traditional socialist orientation, and to model itself after pro-business Democrats in America. As a result, even such post-World War II institutions as the National Health Service (a wide-ranging system of socialist medicine created when the Labor Party was in power) have been undergoing a controversial dismantling in favor of market-oriented, competition-driven procedures. As a result, doctors and hospitals are being forced to function more like private, for-profit businesses than government agencies operating with blank checkbooks.

The Special Relationship

By an early age, virtually every British student knows what the Special Relationship is — the intertwined strands of the cultural, social, political, commercial, historical and moral bonds between the U.K. and the U.S. Relations between the two countries were strengthened during both World Wars, the Korean conflict and the Persian Gulf War. And the U.S. is the U.K.'s most important investment partner. Each pumps approximately US$96 billion into the other's economy annually.

The British realize, intellectually, that their "days of empire" are long gone and that they no longer rule the world's most powerful nation; and they're willing to tacitly concede that title to the United States. However, they cling to the notion that they sit at the United States' right hand — always able to catch Uncle Sam's eye or ear as necessary, in order to keep him on the right track, at least in terms of foreign policy.

The idea of the special relationship flows over from government into business, with the British truly believing that Americans should prefer do business with them, and in their way. It's sometimes a shock to British businesspeople, just as it is to British schoolchildren, to learn that few Americans know (or care) what the Special Relationship is.

7 The Work Environment

The Role of Education

Historically, the working classes were given a basic education that emphasized the battles that built the empire, and perhaps some technical training, if needed, later on. The upper classes went on to university, though even the most privileged seem to view education less as something valuable for its own sake than as something to be gotten through in order to maintain a certain social standing.

As a result, good university education in Britain focused on the classics, rather than on the practical. While knowing how to read Greek or Latin is probably not valuable to today's new business graduate, getting a top degree (a *first*) in the classics from Oxford or Cambridge tells potential employers that the graduate is smart enough to become, with training, a budding banker.

As a result of the Thatcher revolution at home and competition in the marketplace around the world, there has been a rise in the number of professional schools, particularly post-graduate programs offering masters degrees in business administration. The British, both landed gentry and bootstrappers, are realizing that in order to do business internationally, they need to know the language and culture of international business.

The British Work Ethic

The British do what has to be done, and usually apply themselves willingly and well. But they hate to appear eager or hardworking while doing so. They find the American obsession with efficiency, cost effectiveness, "hard sells" and aggressive profitmaking distasteful (and they tend to spend their earnings on fewer material possessions). The best work is accomplished with a sense of effortlessness.

This attitude, like so many others in Britain, is changing gradually, particularly in the financial community, where hustle, aggression and desire are being recognized as critical to success. That's the odd British mix: not wanting to appear as if they're working too hard, but at the same time, not wanting to appear as if they're enjoying life too much.

Status in the Workplace

Vestiges of the class system (as epitomized in the hugely successful television series *Upstairs Downstairs*) are widespread in the British workplace. They can be seen in virtually every office, with the pecking order rising from clerks and tea ladies up to the drones who produce the work, and then up again to the bosses who indulge in long lunches. In the office, as out on the street, there is a way of speaking to others — patronizingly, with equality or subserviently — that depends on the other person's status, relative to one's own. A working-class person (a bartender, for example, or a news agent who sells the banker his daily paper) may be jocular or friendly, but never personally familiar.

Seniority

There's considerable deference in Britain to age and seniority, two of the pillars of the class system, which had its roots in feudalism. Under that medieval system, a worker's future (both poor country laborers and educated urban heirs) depended on the favor of the father figure who presided over the estate or ran the business. Indeed, much of the respect for seniority and age comes from the fact that many large British businesses were founded as family enterprises. Offspring who stood to inherit the reins, but who would not or could not abide by the seniority system, were shipped off to India or Australia or America.

But the Thatcher-inspired emphasis on merit and productivity has gradually weakened some of the old class system's ironclad respect for seniority, particularly among today's self-made entrepreneurs.

Apprenticeship

For centuries, the only way for those not born into the upper classes to improve their lot in life was through a period of servitude to a mentor, who could teach them a craft or trade. Even now, in many British businesses, bright university graduates with no apparent aptitude or experience in a particular field are hired by leading companies to serve as trainees (for anywhere from months to years). They are, in effect, highly paid, professional-management apprentices, and if they keep their noses clean — and show respect to the senior managers and professionals they work with and for — their futures are probably assured.

Hierarchy

In Britain, the boss is the boss. Britons are comfortable knowing where they stand. Look at any London bus stop; people naturally form a *queue* (line), even if it means some of them have to stand in the rain. Similarly, at work, a pecking order is something Britons naturally recognize (or create in their own minds, if necessary). They like working in teams and have a strong sense of fair play. While opinions are encouraged, consensus is very important. They're comfortable giving orders to those below, and taking them from those above. They appreciate polite treatment and being consulted by superiors, but they don't necessarily need or expect it. Many younger workers, however, do like to feel as if they're partners in achieving a business's common goal, rather than just a cog in a clearly defined hierarchy.

Decision Making

As a result of the British respect for hierarchy, decision making is typically a top-down process. Most big public companies feature a board that consults with a chairman to determine overall corporate strategy. In some companies, a strong chairman may dominate the chief executive officer; in others, the CEO will be the most important figure, both in terms of day-to-day operations and long-range strategy.

Memos and meetings are the principal ways with which managers gather information to make decisions. However, at the highest levels of corporate life, the old boy network — still strong, due to its roots in the old class system — can give more weight to a well-placed wink, nudge or quiet word than to the best-reasoned memo from an underling.

Meetings, which are used by some forward-thinking companies as forums to share information, are more often than not called to make assignments for upcoming projects or to review what went wrong on past projects.

When decisions have been made, they are usually final. Few British companies have easy channels for challenging decisions once they've been handed down.

Middle-Level Managers

British middle-level managers may not be an endangered species yet, but they're certainly under threat. In the interests of streamlining and cutting costs, British companies are increasingly scrutinizing their managers for evidence of bottom-line productivity. It's no longer enough to be seen as effective at passing along orders from the decision-makers to the people who carry them out. If they don't actually make a contribution, they're out. With what appears to be a relatively large middle management in many companies, considerable downsizing in Britain is inevitable in the next few years. Forgive British middle managers, then, for being nervous. In fact, avoid them if you can, unless you're offering them an opportunity to enhance their image of irreplaceability within their companies. This enhancement most often takes the form of new services — programs that will save the company money or that will open up new business opportunities.

Women in Business

Generational Shift

Historically, British women spent their time raising children and walking to the local *high street* (main street) to buy daily rations of meat, vegetables and bread. Today, more women are working, and some of them are holding decidedly nontraditional jobs — from taxi drivers to chief financial officers. Surveys show that British men are not eager to share equally in the housework, and anecdotal evidence indicates that many of them still have difficulty taking direction from a female boss or manager.

Britain is still very much a man's world, with the old boy network still ruling over government, industry and business. (Former Prime Minister Margaret Thatcher is the outstanding exception to the rule. It's noteworthy that her successor in 1990, John Major, omitted women from his cabinet.) As in many other countries, however, there is a generational divide: younger men are often much more amenable to working with women than older men. Not that there is always an obvious disrespect or disregard for the skills of working women. It's just that many British businessmen of a certain age and social status approach anyone who is not "one of us" with the same aloofness and vague mistrust.

However, the emphasis is on change. As opportunities for British women gradually increase, British men are learning to live with it, and even to take on traditional female roles themselves — whether working as nurses or doing the family laundry on Saturday mornings.

Working women are entitled to a maximum of eighteen weeks maternity leave (more than France, Germany or the U.S., but less than Italy). Most receive weekly benefits (other than salary) from employers based on up to 90 percent of their average earnings for six weeks, and about US$85 per week for the next twelve.

In Process: New Girl Network

Women constitute almost half the work force, and the most visible among them are entrepreneurs (often involved in some aspect of consumer retailing) or women who work in support positions (often in finance, marketing or communications).

Some cracks are showing in the so-called "glass ceiling" that excludes women from top management position — but not many. And it doesn't appear that that will change significantly in the near future.

Interestingly, many British women are creating their own version of the old boy network, with an emphasis on mutual support and networking for causes ranging from more job opportunities to company-supported day-care centers.

Late-Night Shopping — A New Trend

The expansion of the female work force has created changes throughout British society. One of the biggest has been in the transformation of the retail sector. Not so long ago, late-night shopping in Britain meant the one evening a week when some of the shops stayed open until 8 P.M. Now, most Britons can buy groceries or clothes or auto supplies until 8 or 9 P.M. most evenings, and many superstores — large emporiums that sell groceries, hardware supplies, home furnishings and dry goods all under one roof — routinely stay open until 11 P.M. And after centuries of "blue laws" that kept most stores closed from Saturday afternoon until Monday morning, Sunday shopping has become fairly commonplace. Delivery services and mail order are two other areas that have boomed in recent years, as more British households have two full-time wage earners, neither of whom has the time to run errands during the day.

Strategies for Businesswomen

After being ruled by a woman as dynamic as Margaret Thatcher in the 1980s, it is remarkable that British women haven't progressed farther in business. However, it's been said that Britain is at least ten years behind the United States in terms of feminism in general and business opportunities for women in particular.

Foreign women doing business in Britain need to strike a series of balances. On the one hand, don't try to be one of the good old boys; you'll inevitably look, and probably feel, foolish. On the other hand, don't try to be too feminine; flirts may find British men reluctant to think of them in any other way. At the same time, a hard-edge, all-business facade may be seen as stern or brusque, and too mannish. Finding the right balance may prove difficult, particularly when dealing with the many British businessmen who interpret any sort of assertiveness as overt aggression.

Keep an open mind. The discrimination you feel may be due to the fact that you're foreign, rather than female. But that doesn't make apparent patronizing or condescending behavior or comments any easier to take. Even experienced British businessmen sometimes assume that the woman in the group must be there to take notes, or at best, is a communications or public relations manager. More difficult than the obvious slights are the instances when visiting businesswomen sense that British businessmen are merely biding their time until they can get to speak with the woman's boss — a man, presumably — and really get down to business.

Here's an important tip for dealing with British businesswomen: if you don't know which honorific (Mrs. Miss, Ms.) a woman prefers, don't assume that it's permissible to address her, either in speech or on paper, as Ms. The vast majority of British women use Miss or Mrs. The woman in question may be offended and she will, at the very least, categorize you as presumptive.

9 Making Connections

One of Us?

One of Margaret Thatcher's most famous quotes, spoken when considering the future of a rising young political star, was "Is he one of us?" It is a question that is asked, sometimes openly and sometimes not, throughout the course of daily business dealings in Britain. Though things have changed as a direct result of Thatcher's revolution to create open markets and a new class of entrepreneurs, British business is still dominated by people who speak with the right accent, know the right people, have the right skin color, went to the right schools (preferably Oxford or Cambridge) and share the same right attitudes. (Often as not, "right" means both correct and conservative, with and without the capital C.)

However, those who fit the bill aren't always exempt from discrimination. The knock on them may be nothing more than that they "lifted themselves up by their own bootstraps," instead of being born into an upper-class family with a long history of success and service to crown and country. "He's from up Norf," with the emphasis on the satirical downmarket mis-pronunciation, or "She's an East End girl, of course," is a knowing way of saying that while someone may seem to be one of us, they never really can be.

All of this makes things particularly difficult for foreigners who wish to establish business connections. Needless to say, it helps if they speak English and understand Anglo-American accounting standards. On the positive side, these obstacles become smaller as a Briton recognizes an opportunity to make money.

Business Versus Personal Friendships

While establishing and cultivating working relationships, either friendly or formal, is not as important as in some other countries, the right connections do matter in Britain. Who you know can be more important than what you know. British businesspeople really do say, "Any friend of his is a friend of mine."

At the same time, there is a definite distinction between business friendships and personal ones. Just because a business relationship involves considerable socializing, even between respective family members, it doesn't mean that the friendship extends beyond business matters. Anyone who makes that assumption (however unwittingly) before a Briton is ready risks damaging the business relationship.

The Non-English Advantage

Like most countries in the new global economy, Britain has become more transactional. In the past, companies remained loyal to longtime business associations, even if someone else offered a lower price or a better deal. But with today's emphasis on the bottom line, coupled with fierce worldwide competition in virtually all industries, old loyalties are likely to be tossed on the trash heap. Britons recognize their need for more information and more contacts — new business relationships, in other words. As a result, British business is becoming more open to foreign partnerships.

And, as is often the case in other cultures, the British aren't hampered by the biases that color their relationships with fellow Britons. In some ways, it's easier for them to do business with a French woman or a Texan wearing cowboy boots and a ten-gallon hat than it is with someone who attended a second-rate English private school.

The Proper Introduction

Many Britons, whether in a social or business setting, feel awkward speaking with someone to whom they haven't been formally introduced. This is especially true of older, more traditional managers and professionals. (And even if they *are* willing to stand and chat over drinks with a stranger, the chances are that it won't occur to them to introduce themselves to you.) Keep this in mind when wandering up to people and initiating a conversation. While such behavior is expected in some countries, some Brits may become cool and aloof, if not prickly and rude. If there's someone you wish to meet, find a third party to introduce you. As a last resort, introduce yourself — but with apologies for doing so, expressions about how much you admire the person, and explanations of how much you want to talk to him or her.

The Go-Between

The British have a long tradition of making introductions and finding partners, employees and employers for each other. It actually still happens sometimes in those musty old clubs where geezers — young and old — sit in overstuffed leather chairs reading the latest cricket scores while sipping gin and tonics. Introductions also take place in noisy after-work wine bars, in corporate dining rooms, at race tracks, on trading floors or over business lunches. From street-smart young hustlers, to well-educated, well-spoken, well-connected go-betweens, many Britons earn their living by facilitating these business connections and collecting a cut of the pie. As in other countries, they often prefer to be called "consultants."

Written Introductions

The courtly, seemingly old-fashioned tradition known as "the written introduction" still has its place in Britain, particularly when dealing with old-line companies and long-established professionals (bankers, lawyers). Typically, a go-between would call and say, "I'm sending someone over whom I'd like you to meet. I'll send a letter of introduction." The letter may come separately, or be hand-delivered by the introductee.

Many Britons consider written introductions quaint and would never expect or require one from another British person, much less from a foreigner. But many British managers and professionals like the idea, even if it is merely a formality. After all, quaintness and tradition may not be as revered as they once were, but they still carry some weight. Use your discretion. Some British managers may wonder why the introduction wasn't made in a personal phone call, in a fax or by e-mail.

A Note on British Telephones

Telephones are used more for arranging meetings than for conducting actual business.

When a British telephone rings, it's often a short double ring. When calling a British number, some foreigners get confused by the tones. A relatively long tone, followed by silence, then another relatively long tone, means the phone is ringing. A busy number will have a faster and more constant beep-beep-beep. Many phone numbers have a four-digit area code (for example, 0171 is for central London, 0181 for outlying London numbers), followed by a seven-digit number. Outlying rural areas may feature longer area codes or prefixes and shorter local numbers. (Note: When dialing the U.K. from another country, omit the first "0" in the area code.)

Pay phones are relatively hard to find in many areas. If you need to make lots of calls from the street, it might be wise to stop into a news agent's, pharmacy or candy store and buy a phone card. Many pay phones accept these cards but not money. The old-fashioned red telephone booths may be quaint, but they can also be maddening. In some, you dial the number, and then stand poised with your coins ready to slam into the appropriate slot. If you're not quick enough, you can hear the person on the other end saying, "Hello? Hello" just before you're disconnected. Try again. When you get through, explain that you're at a phone box. Everyone understands.

 Strategies for Success

While many Britons are gregarious, others are likely to be a little aloof — well, more than a little. It's rare to find a Briton who absolutely must establish a personal relationship with someone before discussing business, but certainly he or she will be more comfortable working with people they like and trust. One of the biggest mistakes foreigners can make is to assume that they know British culture and customs, that they can tell what Britons are thinking, or that they know how a deal must play out. The British hate assumptions, sometimes even their own.

British Humor

The British don't tend to appreciate jokes made by non-Brits about the royal family, politics or religion. But they do like wry twists of language and comments about life's absurdities. They often excel at satire, tongue-in-cheek wit and irony. So it's disarming for them to hear Americans — whom they believe are, for the most part, linguistic heathens incapable of irony — say things that are obviously intended to express the opposite of their literal meaning.

They love harmless vulgarisms and find some aspects of American English very colorful. "When he started out, he didn't have a pot to piss in," is an example of a turn of phrase that will elicit an appreciative smile from a British listener who hasn't heard it before.

In a business situation, mild irony and gentle self-deprecation can work to a foreigner's advantage.

Ten Golden Rules

1. Don't assume a deal will be agreed upon just because it makes sense to you and you're convinced that it's to your British counterparts' advantage.

2. Don't assume that "maybe" means "yes," or that a "yes" today will still mean "yes" tomorrow. Some Britons will say anything to avoid explanation or confrontation at a personal level; they may prefer to give information in writing. "I'm surprised that..." or "Did you really ..." are subtle ways of indicating disapproval.

3. Don't be seduced by a smooth British veneer — clothes, accent, charm and education. Remember that you're operating far from your own cultural touchstones. You may need to do twice as much research on a potential partner as you would at home, even on one who seems perfect.

4. Asking for particular, specific, unpublished information about a company may be seen as prying, particularly if the British think the negotiations have not progressed far enough for you to need that information.

5. If you say you're going to do something (show up at a certain time, send certain information in a fax), do it promptly.

6. Don't say or do things in a business deal in Britain that would make you feel uneasy if you

did them back home. The business culture may be different, but not that different.

7. Don't criticize things you don't understand — such as monarchy, the class system, cricket or anything about the British way of doing business.

8. Avoid being overly familiar (such as assuming someone named William is happy to be called Bill). What seems like normal smiling, laughing and enthusiasm to you may be interpreted as being pushy to the British. Wait for the British to initiate personal conversations; even asking where a Briton went to school, or how much business his company did in the United States last year, might be seen as invasive. Always keep in mind that they have a strong sense of privacy.

9. Refrain from using expressions like "ASAP" and "bottom line."

10. Don't drone on about how things are done better (or worse, more efficiently) in your company or in your country. Don't talk a lot about yourself or your past business deals, no matter how eager you are to impress. You risk being viewed as a braggart and a blowhard.

Business Gifts

Gift-giving is not a common part of doing business in Britain. If a gift is given, it should be something related to the business at hand: a sample product, for example, or an umbrella or pen bearing your company logo. But loading someone down with heavily logoed company gear at a first meeting might be seen as presumptive (what makes this person think I want this junk?), as bribery or as just plain foolishness. If a business relationship has progressed to the point that families are discussed, it is permissible to pass on small business-related gifts for children; sporting goods manufacturers might bring along a few basketball jerseys, while a publisher might offer a sampling of children's books.

If business overlaps into off-hours socializing, small gifts for hosts and hostesses are welcome. Flowers are a safe choice for dinner parties, as long as they're not roses, which are reserved primarily for romance.

11 Time

Deadlines

Punctuality is important to the British, but they're not obsessed with it. They're averse to people who constantly rush around, one eye glued to their wristwatches. Arriving within a few minutes of a scheduled appointment is generally acceptable for most business meetings; try to at least be in the building looking for the elevator (the *lift*) by then. A fifteen- to thirty- minute leeway is not unreasonable for most after-hours socializing.

Deadlines, however, are relatively sacrosanct. Missing a deadline is acceptable only if you've given plenty of advance notice, which has then been acknowledged (no matter how grudgingly) by the other side. Three days is not enough notice to suddenly postpone a deadline that's been lingering for three months; two weeks might be.

Power Dining

If your appointment has been scheduled between 11 A.M. and noon, and if your meeting can be expected to last past 1 P.M., you may be invited to lunch, even if the possibility hadn't been mentioned previously. (And it would be rude to call and say, "Are we having lunch?") This is particularly likely at a company that has a private dining room or that serves meals in conference rooms. But it's dangerous to presume, particularly since a lunch invitation may be formally extended only at the last minute, at the host's whim.

Generally speaking, the British prefer to keep work and personal time separate and therefore dislike the idea of combining food with business. Why spoil the meal? Many particularly despise the idea of "the power breakfast" (maybe because it's supposed to be their favorite, and best, meal of the day) and "the power tea."

Business dinners are often more get-acquainted after-work sessions than opportunities to negotiate. There are no particular taboos against drinking alcohol during business lunches and dinners. Don't feel obliged to follow suit, or to try to keep up. Mineral water is fine.

 Business Meetings

Preparation

Meetings should be arranged as far ahead of time as possible, and even then, some telephoning back and forth may be required to establish the meeting's exact timing. Aides, assistants and secretaries usually handle such scheduling. They talk to you, relay the information to the boss, then get back to you, then confer with the boss again, and so on.

Let your British counterparts know how much time you think you'll need. Sending material in advance is almost always a good idea (though that won't necessarily speed things along), as is confirming the meeting via letter, fax or e-mail. Consider including a rough agenda of the points you want to discuss and what you wish to accomplish. But avoid making it seem as if you plan to be in charge of the meeting. Let the Britons hold the home turf.

Telling Who's Who

Unscheduled and unknown players at British meetings are not unusual. There may be a secretary or a public relations person present, marketing or sales personnel may show up, and possibly a solici-

tor or compliance officer. A continental European —
French, Spanish, Italian — may be on hand to repre-
sent the firm's position in the European Union, or
simply to impress visitors with the fact that this is a
European (rather than strictly British) company.
Don't make assumptions based on age, dress or even
who appears to be in charge. It may take some time
for the various roles and authority figures to reveal
themselves. Instead, wait for opportunities for direct
discussion: if you're still not sure about who's who,
wait until someone makes a point or asks a question,
then address them directly.

Presenting Your Business

Be diffident, but efficient. Don't rush, don't dic-
tate, use hand gestures sparingly, and don't make
large predictions — all traits that the British see as
particularly common among Germans and Americans. If you're running the meeting, or presenting a
portion of it, a few brief, seemingly offhand personal
comments — the weather, your trip — are acceptable. But you don't want to be seen as trying too
hard or as being too casual. When the Britons make
comments or ask questions, take notes — especially
if there are questions you cannot answer immediately, or action points that need to be followed up on.

Concluding the Meeting

Even if the meeting is theirs, Britons may wait
for you to make some definitive move toward ending it. Their reluctance to end a meeting may be a
reluctance to be seen as rude — they don't want to
boot you out — or it may be that ending a meeting is
one of those mild, face-to-face confrontations that
Britons tend to avoid. Don't be abrupt, but if things
have obviously wound down to the point of redun-

dancy and idle chatter, you might announce that you have work to do elsewhere or that you've probably taken up enough of their time for that day.

Ten Meeting Guidelines

1. Arrive a few minutes early, to allow for small talk — nothing too personal.

2. Call the meeting to order within a few minutes of the allotted time. Don't seem rushed or in a hurry.

3. Introduce yourself and your companions, with their respective titles, responsibilities and reasons for attending.

4. Give a brief overview of the subject.

5. Describe what you hope to accomplish, both that day and over the course of time.

6. Run things with casual formality. Be efficient, but not brusque or bossy.

7. Allow plenty of opportunity for questions and comments.

8. At the end, sum up what you think was accomplished and where you think things are heading.

9. Review action points and deadlines, both yours and theirs.

10. Follow up with a note or memo summarizing the meeting.

13 Negotiating with the British

There is no single British negotiation style. The specifics will depend on the industry or business and, to a much larger degree, on the personalities involved. Typically, the British will strive to create a neutral environment conducive to making both parties comfortable. No one will force you into a sauna to try to literally sweat a deal out of you, the way the Finns do. The British will try to anticipate your needs, from food and drink to clerical help, and they'll try to meet any unanticipated needs quickly and efficiently. As a rule, that's how they do business with each other, and they take the same approach with foreigners.

Opening Protocol

The British prefer *tidy* schedules and agendas, and they don't like surprises. If you're running the meeting or it's your time to present, begin by introducing yourself and those with you; include jobs titles and the reason why each of you is present. Lay out the procedural agenda or timetable, and then go through the substantial points, one by one. Point out practical implications and the long-term view. Allow time for questions, either as you move through the presentation, at the end, or both. When you're finished, sum up, propose action points for everyone involved and suggest deadlines, if applicable.

The Negotiation

There is more ice than fire in British negotiations. An absolute, line-in-the-sand refusal to negotiate on any particular point will be viewed as unhelpful, and possibly rude. Allow for concessions. If there's something you must insist on, do so quietly and firmly, not with threats, speeches or ultimatums.

In some parts of the world, negotiators with iron bottoms (those who can sit at the table the longest) are often the winners. While that's sometimes true in Britain, many British think it's vulgar to be deprived of life's necessary comforts — sleep, food, and so on — for the sake of a business deal.

At the same time, they don't like to feel pushed to conclude a deal because of time pressures. If you insist that certain things must be accomplished by a specific time to suit your purposes, you may find the British saying that it's your problem, not theirs.

Ending the Negotiating Session

Negotiations often end with handshakes and an oral agreement, both of which are taken seriously. However, these are not an ironclad indications that the proper contracts will be signed and the deal carried out. Britons may have second thoughts or, more often, they may need to get approval from a boss, partner or board (a fact that they may have failed to mention in the course of the negotiation). In Britain as elsewhere, a deal isn't legally binding until it's been spelled out on paper and signed by all the appropriate parties.

Contracts, British-style

The British like detailed, specific contracts. They also like contracts that are governed by British law and that stipulate that fact. If you're negotiating a contract under which later disputes and disagreements will be determined by British law, be sure to consult a British *solicitor* (a non-trial lawyer) as opposed to a *barrister*, before signing.

Interpreters

While speaking foreign languages is commonplace among businesspeople in some European countries, that's not the case in Britain. The British are notoriously (and in some cases, determinedly) mono-lingual. Their all-too-frequent attitude is that since English is the international business language, all those involved should be fluent in it.

Consequently, non-native English speakers hoping to conduct business in Britain should consider using an interpreter, especially for sensitive negotiations. It's best to arrange for one independently, and well in advance, rather than relying on your British counterparts to find one. Your interpreter should be both multicultural and multilingual, and able to pick up on feelings and intonations in both languages. It's always advisable to have an interpreter whose native language is the same as your own, so that he or she is translating into his or her native tongue, rather than into a second language.

14 Business Outside the Law

Britain's crime rates are lower than those in the United States, but higher than those in Japan or Scandinavia. Violent crimes, especially those involving guns, are relatively rare (firearms are strictly controlled), though much of the country is overrun by pickpockets — especially during the summer in crowded tourist areas. Organized crime exists, but it doesn't have the same sort of ingrained economic and cultural influence as it does in some countries.

Underground Economy

The focus of Britain's underground economy has shifted in recent years from outright illegal contraband (drugs, for example) to the importing of legal goods in quantities that exceed British Customs and Excise quotas. The opening of borders with neighboring countries in the European Union's single market has made it easier to smuggle in vast quantities of beer, wine, liquor and tobacco (both cigarettes and loose tobacco, since many Britons still prefer to roll their own), and thus avoid Britain's luxury taxes.

The Fiddle

Being *on the fiddle* refers to small-time thievery or cheating, usually by employees or small businesses. It is widely believed, for example, that many bartenders are on the fiddle — meaning that they pocket some of the pub's receipts every week. A tradesman who is hired to do some work and overcharges for the materials is *playing a fiddle* on his customer.

Graft and Corruption

The British have their share of embezzlement, fraud and other white-collar crimes, but these tend to stay within national boundaries (except for the occasional foray into illegal arms deals). Many Britons (including leading business executives and politicians) are eager to exploit their positions for personal gain — whether a vacation at a partner's expense or a lucrative personal deal on the side. The important distinction is that such arrangements (such as a member of Parliament being paid extremely well to speak to a group that is lobbying him) are regarded as perks of position, rather than as conflicts of interest. It's rare for a foreigner to be expected to pay bribes or kickbacks in order to do business in the U.K.

Present Changes and Future Outlook

Britain is becoming more and more ethical on several fronts, from stiffer rules governing how politicians can earn outside income to sharper definitions of insider trading. The British pride themselves on their ability to do business around the world, and at the moment, the world business climate is demanding more openness and honesty.

 ## Names & Greetings

Royalty

There are times, both socially and professionally, when foreigners are presented to British royalty. These are usually lesser princes and princesses, or dukes and duchesses — fringe royals who are more active in business (sometimes looking for deals of their own) and in high society (where they're notorious for hating to pay for anything). Even though they aren't part of Buckingham Palace's inner circle, strict protocol prevails. Wait to be introduced. Never speak first. Give a little bow or curtsy if you want to fit in. If you don't bow or curtsy, no one will arrest you, but you probably won't end up involved in long conversations. Not that you'd end up doing so anyway — unless you're offering a really good freebie, or a way for the royal to make some money without working.

Lesser Nobility

Titles still abound in the British upper class, and they still mean something — though not necessarily intelligence or wisdom. Dukes and barons are at the top, followed by various classes of lords and ladies. Some of the prized old lordships are inherited, handed down from generation to generation since the Domesday Book (a record of English landholdings commissioned by William the Conqueror in the year 1086). Their attendant lands and castles are now often opened to the public, whose tour fees help pay for the heating bills.

Some lordships are awarded by the government for long years of service and success — in the military, politics, art, or increasingly, private business. Whether inherited or awarded, lords and ladies are entitled to sit in the House of Lords and vote on the major political issues of the day. They expect to be formally addressed as Lord or Lady, followed by their surname, as in Lord Wedgewood.

Lords of the Manor

Lordships should not be confused with the title "Lord of the Manor." This is an honorary and fairly meaningless title. Many lordships of this stripe are sold at auction, often to Americans, for tens of thousands of dollars. Most lordships of manors carry the name of a place — "The Lord of the Manor of Rossmore," for example, with Rossmore being the name of the nearby village. Most of these lordships lost any legal claims to real property long ago, though a few do still carry centuries-old rights — such as the Lord's right to drive his geese through the village square on market days.

Knights and Dames

Knights and Dames are taken quite seriously. Usually awarded by the government in recognition of extremely successful careers in business, politics, the military or the arts, these titles carry no rights or responsibilities (no voting in the House of Lords or driving geese across the village green). However, they entitle the holder to be known forevermore as Sir or Dame. Well-known honorees include Sir Walter Raleigh (a 17th century navigator), Sir Lawrence Olivier (an actor) and Dame Beatrix Potter (a writer and illustrator).

Common British Business Titles

Aside from royals and other assorted, titled "blue-bloods," stick with Mr. for men and Miss or Mrs. for women. Use Ms. only if it's been specifically requested.

Director is a standard executive title in the U.K. *Managing director* is roughly the equivalent of the U.S. titles president or CEO (chief executive officer).

Some Britons routinely add *Esquire* (or the abbreviation *Esq.*) after men's names, when addressing letters to them. The word originally meant "shield" and was used to indicate that a man was one step away from knighthood (in other words, a shield-bearer in attendance to a knight). Today, it's a politely old-fashioned way of saying Mister.

British people seem more likely than Americans, but less likely than people from many other countries, to call attention to their academic degrees in their business titles. Virtually all Britons with medical degrees expect to be called "doctor," but some Britons with doctorates in philosophy want to be called doctor, too. Make them happy.

First Names

Don't presume to call a Briton by his or her first name without either asking if it's all right, or waiting for him or her to extend the informality first (especially if there's a considerable difference in age and rank and you're on the lower rung).

Also, be careful about overemphasizing British titles, particularly in a business setting. One American company successfully lured several members of the House of Lords to a function, but then blew it by having its employees make them pin on nametags that all had "Lord" printed quite large, with their last names quite small underneath.

Don't assume nicknames are permissible, even nicknames popular in other variations of English, such as American and Australian. Many Britons named Robert, William, Henry or Charles would shudder at being called Bob, Bill, Hank or Chuck.

Business Cards

As with many other things, the British are sometimes self-conscious with business cards. You want their card, they know you want it, they want to give it to you and they want yours. Yet they often wait to be pointedly asked, and then examine the card with a self-conscious muttering about "doing the Japanese ritual" (since they see Asians as compulsive card swappers). Like their money, the cards that many British hand out don't seem to be of any standard size. Some are so large that there's no easy place to carry them. Others are so small, or so oddly proportioned, that they don't fit in with any stack of other business cards. But then, maybe that's the point.

Be cautious about pressing for e-mail addresses; the British did not initially rush to embrace the Internet and the World Wide Web. Some older British businesspeople actually believe that the entire phenomenon is just another American-inspired fad that they have no need to learn about. Asking about doing business via computerized telecommunications may be interpreted as an attempt on your part to seem superior.

 Communication Styles

Nonverbal Communication

British reserve tends to heighten when meeting foreigners. While their communication style relies heavily on the many nuances of English, other subtleties also apply.

The British tend to follow the norms of Western body language: leaning forward shows interest, for example, while leaning back shows disinterest. While crossed legs are seen as a sign of relaxation and a casual attitude, they're only permissible in business settings if one's posture doesn't approach outright lounging.

Small smiles and nods and an occasional "Hmmm" are viewed as positive encouragements to a conversation, but they can mean either enthusiasm for what is being said or a desire for the speaker to hurry up and get it over with. Be wary of large, toothy smiles. The British know that Americans, particularly, think of them as having inferior dental care, so they don't want to show anyone their teeth (and they don't want to see anyone else's, either).

Spitting or blowing one's nose in public is considered vulgar, as is chewing gum in meetings. Smoking is acceptable, as long as it's not over food.

Some Guidelines

The following will help you become more sensitive to your body language and the ways in which it might be interpreted in Britain.

- **Handshake etiquette.** Don't be put off by the relatively weak British handshake. It's nothing personal. Britons see a big, firm handshake as very American, and therefore to be avoided.
- **Don't get physical.** Touching is a form of familiarity, and the British don't surrender their familiarity easily. Backslapping or putting your arm around someone's shoulders, particularly in public, will make many Britons uncomfortable.
- **Never kiss a British woman in a business setting.** Even one of those innocent little kisses that consists of blowing a bit of air past the cheek will be considered, well, *cheeky*.
- **Don't speak loudly, or often.** Foreigners are often regarded as noisy and chatty. Speak in a low, controlled voice.
- **Don't stare.** A direct gaze during business conversations is appropriate, but Britons are disconcerted by a long stare directly into their faces.
- **Honor the queue.** If waiting for something with strangers — for a pay phone, a bus, a bank, a shop, a ticket line, a doctor's office or a restaurant — never *jump* the queue by pushing your way into line. The British naturally *queue up* to patiently wait their turn, and anyone who abuses this custom is regarded as a minor outlaw.
- **Be careful about hand gestures.** Giving the two-finger "V for victory" salute, or holding up two fingers in a restaurant to indicate to a waiter that there are two of you for dinner, are

considered vulgar gestures equivalent to an upraised middle finger in some other countries. If you're in the restaurant situation, make sure that your palm (not the back of your hand) is facing the waiter.

- **A matter of chivalry.** Giving up your seat on the bus or the Underground to someone who needs it — an older person, for example, or a woman in late pregnancy — will probably mark you as a foreigner to the other passengers (and as a hero to the person who needs the seat). Be aware that your gesture may be taken as grandstanding by any British acquaintances you're traveling with (and who never considered giving up *their* seats). Think twice about it, and then do it anyway.

- **Standing introductions.** If someone enters a business meeting, follow the host's lead on whether to stand or not. Typically, you'll stand if it's someone to whom you'll be introduced; if not, you'll remain seated.

- **Leg crossing.** Women should cross their legs at the ankle, not at the knees. Watch for news photos of the Queen.

(Other Queenly protocol includes always traveling with her own toilet seat but never with a passport, feeding her pet dogs from sterling silver trays brought in by a footman, and never carrying money — though British bank notes feature her portrait. She is, by the way, believed to be one of the wealthiest women in the world.)

 Customs

Guy Fawkes, April Fool's & Pancakes

Guy Fawkes Day (November 5) commemorates the foiling of the 1605 Gunpowder Plot to blow up Parliament. Children stuff dummies of Fawkes, stand out on the street and call, "Penny for the Guy!" hoping that passersby will drop coins in a hat or box. That night, they throw their dummies onto huge bonfires and set off fireworks displays.

It's possible that the British embrace April Fool's Day (April 1) with more enthusiasm than any other nation. Even the BBC (British Broadcasting Corporation) and the national newspapers carry outlandish spoofs disguised as straightforward reportage (like a government plan to move Trafalgar Square). All jokes are supposed to end at noon, but keep your wits about you for the rest of the day.

On the day before Lent begins, Britain is awash in pancakes, supposedly to fortify the populace for the weeks of deprivation ahead. Pancake races — with people running down the streets or across playgrounds with pans and pancakes in their hands — are popular.

Blood Sports

Many Britons still regard shooting grouse and "riding to the hounds" as part of their genteel heritage. During the autumn and winter, landed gentry don red coats, mount fine steeds and turn their baying beagles loose on a scared young fox. Then fox, hounds and horses career over the countryside, thrashing through everyone's property (the traditional hunt is why British trespassing laws are relatively lax and rarely enforced). The riders try to intervene before the dogs can tear the cornered fox apart.

In recent years, fox hunts have been enlivened by opposition from "sabs" — hunt saboteurs. In the name of animal rights, sabs spray the woods and fields with the juice of rotting garlic (which prevents the dogs from tracking the fox's scent), or try to catch and rescue the fox themselves or scare away the dogs and horses.

For those who prefer to watch and wager, without the bloodshed, there's the Grand National Steeplechase, Epsom Derby (which attracts over 250,000 spectators), plus dozens of greyhound race tracks.

Christmas

Many Western Christmas traditions are British in origin. *Wassailing* is named for an ancient holiday beverage made of ale, eggs, cream, roasted apples, nuts and spices. Those too poor to make their own wassail went from door to door, singing carols in exchange for some of the brew. (The recipe called for slices of toasted bread to be floated on top, which may be the origin of the expression "to drink a toast.")

Kissing under a sprig of mistletoe is believed to date back to Druid rituals. Massive Yule logs (expected to burn from Christmas Eve until Epiphany on January 6th) warmed the great halls of feudal England, and fragments were saved to light the next year's log. Chimney stockings are said to prevent Father Christmas's gold coins from tumbling down and getting lost in the ash grate.

Henry VIII, Britain's 16th century Tudor king, decorated the royal gardens at Christmas with strings of pearls, silk flowers and pomegranates, and he's said to have dined on spice-stuffed peacock — which had been roasted, sewn back into its plumage and covered with gold leaf.

Decorated evergreens, a German custom, were unknown in the U.K. until 1841, when Prince Albert (himself German) had an enormous tree set up in Windsor Castle to amuse the royal family. The sending of Christmas cards also began in the Victorian era and is attributed to one Sir Henry Cole, the first to produce them commercially (thus taking advantage of the newly established one-penny postal service).

Though Charles Dickens' ever-popular *A Christmas Carol* glorifies goose, turkey is the traditional fare for big family holiday meals today, with a plum pudding for dessert. (The name refers back to a time before prunes had been replaced by raisins.) *Christmas crackers* (small, gaily wrapped cardboard cylinders) are laid on each plate. Diners cross arms so that each person is holding one end of his or her cracker, and one end of a neighbor's. Everyone yanks at once. The tiny amount of gunpowder pops to reveal cheap toys, flimsy paper crowns and little strips of paper on which are printed extraordinarily bad puns.

Some families close the holiday season with a Twelfth Night Cake. Favors (a bean, a coin, a button) are mixed into the sweet batter before baking

— symbols of what the new year will bring (wisdom, wealth, faithfulness).

If you don't mind being part of an enormous human crush, consider joining one of the public gatherings — complete with noise makers, pealing church bells and thousands of voices singing *Auld Lang Syne* together — that usher in the New Year in Glasgow, Edinburgh or London's Trafalgar Square.

Weddings

British wedding receptions feature a series of toasts that often escalate into increasingly ribald verbal jousts between the sexes. (Never try to join in and give a toast without being invited first. It isn't done.) Sometimes there's dancing, usually there's lots of food. The wedding cake is often a hard, heavy fruit cake, covered with thick layers of tough frosting; it's not unusual for the bride and groom to be unable to cut it without the assistance of able-bodied hotel or restaurant employees armed with extra-large, extra-sharp knives. No one leaves the reception until the newlyweds depart for their honeymoon — which means that if the couple stays too long, guests who want to head home may get grumpy, but if they leave too early, they risk missing the best part of their own party.

Gardening

The British are fanatical gardeners. During the 18th century, whole villages were removed to make way for them, and in the 19th century, flower seeds and cuttings began arriving from around the world: dahlias from Mexico, tea-scented roses from China. Knot gardens and labyrinthine maze gardens were carefully clipped into elaborate geometric shapes. The wealthy augmented their acres of greenery with trellised pavilions, Chinese temples and bridges, Egyptian archways and seashell-encrusted grottos. Baron Ferdinand de Rothschild had parrots placed on stands on his Mentmore estate, which had been planted so that the flowers matched the birds' feathers.

Today, programs about gardening are among the highest-rated on the main television channels and are routinely shown during prime time viewing hours. Even in the most crowded urban areas, people spend hours cultivating flower boxes, slaving over tiny squares of dirt outside their back doors, or training vines to grow a certain way. A popular weekend day out is to visit one or more of Britain's 3,600 public gardens or the manicured grounds of a private estate.

D.I.Y.

Do It Yourself. If gardening is the great British outdoor preoccupation, then D.I.Y. — fixing up the house — is its indoor equivalent. A common reply when someone is asked what he or she did over the weekend is, "A spot of D.I.Y."

Labor rates (for plumbers, carpenters, electricians and the like) are high, and weekend service is almost impossible to find. D.I.Y. stores (some of them are enormous) sell the tools, paint and other supplies that feed the national desire to paper walls, tile bathrooms, strip furniture, hang shelves, seal doors against drafts, pave garden paths, replace fixtures and so on. D.I.Y. magazines offer suggestions and reassurance.

 Dress & Appearance

Business Attire

The British dress for business (that is, conservatively) and expect you to do the same. Even male artists and designers who favor ponytails and earrings put on ties and jackets for important meetings.

Pastels tend to look out of place at a London business meeting, even on a rare, hot August afternoon. Umbrellas (they're called *brollies* but sadly, they're rarely set off by a bowler hat anymore) are a popular, year-round fashion accessory, as are raincoats and well-made briefcases.

For Men

Charcoal, gray and dark blue dominate in men's suiting. Ties have been getting wider and more colorful, but they're still not as splashy as those in other countries. Be wary of striped ties; they may be similar in color and pattern to those favored for school and regimental uniforms, and people may think it curious for a foreigner to wear an old school tie from a place he didn't even attend. Shirts with button-down collars are not unheard of, but they're regarded as a primarily American affectation. A watch and a ring or two are the extent of the jewelry for most men, though little lapel pins — sometimes remarkably whimsical — are common.

For Women

Trousers (don't call them "pants" — that means underwear, also known as *knickers*) are relatively rare among professional and management types, though common among secretaries, personal assistants and other nonprofessional support staff. Women executives are expected to dress much like men, in sober, conservative suits. In spring and summer, however, the occasional brightly colored jacket is acceptable, as long as there are no big meetings scheduled that day. Many women in Britain like to offset the mannish styles with a small flutter of feminine fashion, such as a scarf or a bit of frill on a blouse.

Suspenders versus Braces

The suspenders that hold up a man's trousers are called *braces*. *Suspenders* to the British are the clips that dangle from a lady's garter belt to hold up her stockings. Many British women still prefer to buy stockings by the pair, rather than to wear panty hose.

Fancy Dress

If you receive an invitation that reads "Smoking," it means that men are required to wear *dinner jackets* (tuxedos) and women, long dresses.

For weddings, women favor hats, particularly if the ceremony takes place in a church or outside in a country garden. Middle- and upper-middle-class men often wear traditional morning coats, complete with striped trousers, *waistcoats* (decorative vests) and gray top hats.

 Reading the British

A poker face sometimes accompanies the traditional stiff upper lip, and the combination makes the British difficult to read. They like it that way. Perhaps it's become ingrained with all those centuries of military and commercial empire-building, but showing emotion is regarded as a weakness (particularly in business), and so is letting other people know more than they need to know at any one time.

Understatement is the preferred manner of communication. Listen carefully for what may seem like mild, wry observations. In countries devoted to a more blunt and open style of doing business, such comments may be viewed as little jokes. In Britain, they may be the best indication you'll get of the real feelings of the British person you're dealing with. "Bloody nuisance, that clause," uttered by a Briton, might be interpreted as a throwaway line, an offhand, inconsequential remark by an American. But to the Briton who said it, it was akin to all but shouting that a potential deal is doomed unless changes are made in the offending clause.

Gestures and Expressions

Dealing with a topic very quickly and then dismissing it from the conversation can mean either that the Briton is in full agreement and the outcome is a foregone conclusion, or that the Briton disagrees so vehemently that it's not worth discussing. Certainly looking away and shuffling papers indicates discomfort with the way things are going.

Tapping the side of one's nose with a finger indicates secrecy or confidentiality. Many Brits have very fair complexions, making them vulnerable to a tell-tale flushed face when embarrassed, angry or otherwise unsettled.

Business Clichés

These phrases are often heard in British business conversations:

- **At the end of the day** ("After all is said and done"). As in, "At the end of the day, this is what's required..."
- **A level playing field** (fairness). As in, "All we ask is for a level playing field with our competitors..."
- **A sea change** (a radical, fundamental change). As in, "We're not asking for a sea change here, but we do want to make this minor modification..."

20 Socializing

British invitations often carry the phrasing, *6:30 for 7 o'clock*, or *12:30 for 1 o'clock*. The first time mentioned is for drinks and socializing, while the second time is for eating, usually a sit-down dinner but sometimes a buffet. Skipping the cocktail period in big groups is permissible, but can be risky in small groups where your absence would be noticed. Have a good excuse ready, and use it freely, with apologies.

Small Talk

The weather, very changeable but rarely extreme, is the touchstone of British small talk, particularly in business settings. Try to keep your comments centered on the *British* weather; tales of waist-deep snows, torrential floods or searing heat back home may strike the British as bragging on your part. Even worse, they may think you're saying that their weather isn't very interesting in comparison.

Animals are probably the second-safest topic. The English love most creatures that fly, swim or walk on all fours. Some they shoot, snare or hook, others they groom and put on show, still others sleep in their parlors.

The Conversational Mine Field

Many Britons will try to sound out a for-eigner's political leanings in a way that would seem intrusive if they did it with another Briton. They are particularly interested in American poli-tics, and will ask pointed questions that often show — and may be designed to show — that they know as much or more about the current U.S. political scene than the visiting American does. Try to remain nonpartisan and to defend the American system in general; otherwise, you may find your-self having to defend politicians you don't neces-sarily like yourself.

Most questions about the decline of empire, the role of the royalty (and its recent litany of scandals), the class system or what's happening in Northern Ireland will be viewed as an inherent criticism. Other sensitive topics include religion, sexuality, greasy food, smoking and poor service. The British know that their country has many shortcomings, but they don't like to be put in the position of hav-ing to defend or explain them.

If a person happens to say he is a Tory, he proba-bly regards himself as upper class; if he says he is a Conservative, he probably regards himself as middle class. And if he says he is a Socialist, he probably regards himself as an upper-class supporter of the Labor Party. Most others who identify themselves as members of the Labor Party probably think of them-selves as middle class or working class.

Weekending

British executives who might never think of inviting you home for dinner (too intimate) might be willing, even eager, to spend an entire weekend with you at their country house. Be prepared for any sort of activity, from helping to clear out a fish pond or weed a garden to a semi-formal dinner party after a day of shooting grouse or *riding to the hounds*. Go ahead and ask what sort of clothing you might need. If the response is "Not to worry," it means that they probably have mud rooms full of *wellies* (knee-high boots, named after the first Duke of Wellington) and *macintoshes* (raincoats, named after the 19th century Scottish chemist who invented rubberized cotton) for guests who need them.

Feel free to take a nice gift along: nothing too ostentatious, but something luxurious enough for everyone to enjoy, such as fancy chocolates, good cigars or expensive wine. Flowers are fine, but avoid giving white lilies (associated with funerals) or roses (symbolic of romance).

Events

Annual sporting, social and charity events often tie into business entertaining in Britain. There's the Henley Royal Regatta on the Thames, a tradition since 1829 (white trousers, striped blazers and picnic baskets are the norm). At the Ascot horse races, a favorite of the royal family, ladies are expected to wear hats, and entry to certain areas will be refused to those wearing short skirts or, God forbid, trousers. If you're invited to Centre Court at Wimbledon and have never been to a top-flight professional tennis tournament, brush up on the etiquette of when you're allowed to talk, stand up or leave your seat to go to the lavatory, so you won't be seen as an idiot — or *wally*, as the British say.

If you're playing a sport rather than just watching one, remember that trying too hard to win is not always seen as sporting; think twice about cranking that first serve toward the weaker opponent during a friendly game of mixed doubles. If someone hits a poor shot in tennis, golf or croquet or otherwise has a sporting failure, the proper comment is "Bad luck!" A soft rain usually doesn't interrupt play, casual or otherwise; the British have learned that if they waited for perfect weather, they'd never play at all.

If you're hoping to playing nine or eighteen holes of golf (St. Andrew's in Scotland is world famous), you may be required to prove your handicap beforehand, preferably with a letter obtained from the pro or secretary at your home course.

In the Limelight

Shakespeare's legacy is alive and well in the guise of the Royal Shakespeare Company, and London's West End theater district has an international following. Two or three dozen plays may be running on any given evening, and tickets for hit shows (such as *Cats, Evita* or *Phantom of the Opera*, all by the prolific Andrew Lloyd Webber) sell out months in advance. Be warned. Most performances begin at 8 P.M., and latecomers may be required to sit in the lobby until intermission. Excellent theaters can also be found in Hampstead, Hammersmith and Wimbledon.

Pubs

The pub (short for "public house") is the cornerstone of British social life, and it serves many purposes — from a place to unwind after work for professionals to an extension of one's living rooms for working types. There are about 80,000 of them scattered throughout the United Kingdom; some date back to the 15th century. Don't turn down an invitation to one just because you don't drink; you're more likely to strike up a conversation with a local here than elsewhere. And keep in mind that British *beer* (usually in the form of *stout, bitter, mild* or *pale ale*) is served at a cool room temperature, while *lager* is served chilled. *Cider* is an alcoholic brew of fermented apple or pear juice.

Bartenders don't expect tips, and may be miffed if you leave money on the bar; it means they have to come out from behind the bar to return it to you, thinking you left it inadvertently. Table service is rare, even where food is served. Drinks are typically ordered in *rounds*, with drinkers taking turns buying for everyone at the table. Even if you're not drinking, don't miss an opportunity to buy — or at least offer to buy — a round. If you're not drinking, and the conversation is deteriorating (often after three or four rounds of pints), feel free to excuse yourself. The important thing is that you went to the pub, not that you stayed to the bitter (pun intended) end.

Political Beers

Recently, the Scots have taken to advertising their political beliefs via their local brews. These include "Rutland Independence Ale" to celebrate the re-establishment of Rutland as England's smallest county; "Independence Ale," a paean to Scottish nationalists; and "Extortion Ale," a protest against the high tolls being charged on a bridge near the brewery site.

Other beers on the market cater to environmentalists, homosexuals and lesbians, and one commemorates an 18th century pledge to keep the gates of a particular ancestral home closed until a Stuart is restored to Britain's throne.

21 Entertaining

Tea, the National Drink

"What would the world do without tea?" wrote Sidney Smith, an 18th century British evangelist. "How did it exist [before]?"

The Dutch first brought tea to Europe via China in 1610. King Charles II, having grown up in exile at The Hague (because his father, Charles I, had been beheaded by Cromwell), brought home a taste for the leafy beverage. Touted as a panacea for everything from epilepsy and consumption to paralysis and vertigo, it soon became a trend among London's high society. ("It easeth the Brain, strengtheneth the Memory, overcometh superfluous Sleep ... and removeth obstructions of the Spleen," claimed one enterprising purveyor.) By 1725, England was importing a quarter of a million pounds of *tay* (as it was called then) annually; one local complained that "as much superfluous money is expended on tea and sugar as would maintain 4 million more subjects on bread." By 1800, the figure had risen to 24 million pounds. "Though ridiculed by those ... not susceptible of influence from so refined a stimulant," wrote English author Thomas De Quincey (1785–1859), "[tea] will always be the favored beverage of the intellectual."

The well-to-do began gathering in "tea gardens," outdoor expanses of arbors and flowered walks where they could take tea together, listen to concerts and sometimes watch fireworks. But it wasn't until India became a British colony (and the British realized, to their astonishment, that tea plants could not only be grown in, but were actually indigenous to, the jungles of Assam) that the drink became affordable to every level of society. By 1939, the United Kingdom was importing 469 million pounds of the stuff.

Today, tea is drunk all day long, but especially in the afternoon; the average Briton drinks three cups a day. There is a real ritual to the *cuppa* in many homes; loose tea (Earl Grey, English Breakfast, Lapsang Souchang) is brewed and steeped in a teapot covered with a cloth sleeve (a *cosy*), then strained into cups that have been rinsed with hot water to take the chill off. Tea is sometimes served with lemon, but more often with milk. *White tea* contains a double or triple shot of milk.

Elevenses, Cream Tea & High Tea

Many Britons take a break in their routines around 11 A.M. known as "elevenses" for a cup of tea, coffee, a soda or even a candy bar.

Afternoon Tea was the brainchild of Anna, the seventh Duchess of Bedford. In the late 1700s, huge breakfasts and late suppers were customary, and by 5 o'clock, the duchess suffered what she called "a sinking feeling." So she ordered tea and cakes to be served. It became an aristocratic fashion and then a national habit. Today, *afternoon tea* might include crustless cucumber or watercress sandwiches, pastries and *biscuits* (cookies). *Cream Tea* includes fresh scones — you cut them in half, slather on clotted cream, top with a dollop of fruit jam, and then try to eat before you hear your arteries creaking shut.

If a Briton refers to "being mother" or "playing mother," he or she is referring to the one who will pour the tea for everyone else.

What used to be called *High Tea* in many households is more of a marketing gimmick used by fancy hotels to attract foreign customers, who think that sounds more regal or luxurious. In fact, the traditional high tea was usually a 6 P.M. supper for children and the working classes: meat, vegetables, bread, dessert and a beverage (which may or may not have been tea).

Sunday Lunch

Sunday lunch is typically a huge feast heavy with red meat (though roast beef has declined in popularity since the Mad Cow Disease scare of early 1996), roast potatoes, peas and carrots and a sweet dessert. In many households, the men gather in the local pub to down a pint or three while the women stay home and cook, then they all sit down together in the mid- to late afternoon.

If you're hoping for such traditional English marvels as eel and mash pie, venison pasties or whelks and local shellfish, you'll probably be disappointed.

Table Manners

The British hold the fork in the left hand and the knife in the right hand, and they don't switch the fork from the left hand to the right before taking it to the mouth. But they don't mind if you do. They may be alarmed, however, if you tip your soup bowl toward you when finishing it off. If you must tip it at all, tip it away from you. This habit originated with their seagoing tradition; when dining on a ship, a sudden swaying from a big wave could put the soup in your lap.

Here are a few tips on table etiquette:

- Don't lean with your elbows on the table.

- The salad often comes after the main course, not before.

- A cheese course may be served before or after or instead of dessert.

- *Pudding* could turn out to be a savory (such as Yorkshire or blood pudding), a cake, a tart or a pastry.

- When coffee is offered after a meal, you can ask for decaf, but don't be disappointed if it's not available. And be aware that you may be stereotyped as a health nut.

- Before or after the coffee, port is sometimes served. Treat this sweet, strong wine with caution. The British are used to it, but many a visitor has found himself — or herself — saying things late in the evening that were better left unsaid.

When You're the Host

If you're dealing with a Briton on an even footing, and want to keep it that way, make sure you take your turn at issuing invitations and offering to pay the check (the *bill*). Be aware that transportation is a consideration. In some situations, particularly with more senior managers, they may not be willing (or indeed, able) to arrange for their own train, bus or taxi. Sending a car or personally picking up a high-ranking executive may even be expected.

Many better British restaurants are used to business clientele; calling in advance to request a certain seating arrangement or table, particularly one that affords quiet conversation, is advisable.

Toasting & Tipping

If you're hosting any sort of occasion, even a dinner, it's often expected that you 'll make a toast to start the drinking, even if it's just to raise your glass and say, "Cheers!"

Many guests wouldn't dream of starting to eat a course until the host begins, especially if the host is a woman. But don't start before everyone has been served (or everyone at your table, if it's a large gathering).

At formal dinners, the Loyal Toast (a toast to Her Majesty's health) may be offered after the main course. For those who smoke during meals, be aware that it's considered a great breach of etiquette to light a cigarette before the Loyal Toast is over.

If you're paying, a tip of 10 to 15 percent is standard, more for extraordinary service — though many Britons think 15 percent is needlessly extravagant.

22 Basic British Phrases

British versus American English

Between 3,000 and 4,000 different words and phrases distinguish North American from British English. For example, potato *chips* in American English are *crisps* in Britain, where *chips* are french fries. To the British, a car's trunk and hood are the *boot* and *bonnet*, gasoline is *petrol*, the radio is the *wireless* and the drugstore is the *chemist*.

Consequently, there's plenty of room for confusion in what George Bernard Shaw called "a common culture separated only by its common language." In Britain, *to table* something means to discuss it immediately (that is, to put it on the table), whereas in the U.S. it means putting something aside until an unspecified future date. (This particular difference in meaning has caused more than one business deal to go under.) Similarly, to "slate" something in the U.K. means to criticize it, while in the U.S. it means to put it on the schedule. And if someone requests a *rubber* (American slang for a condom), he wants an eraser. In Britain, *knocking someone up* means paying them a visit, whereas in American slang, it means getting someone (probably not your wife) pregnant.

A bathroom is the room reserved for taking baths. If a Briton asks for *the smallest room in the house* or the *W.C.* (water closet), he's looking for the toilet (*loo* in slang, *bog* in crude slang). When angry, don't say you're *really pissed*; it means drunk. Scotch whisky is just plain *whisky*, and English muffins are just plain *muffins*. When the British move, they *move house*, and when they're in the hospital, they are *in hospital*.

Spellings also vary. Words ending in *-or* in American, for example, end in *-our* in British: color and colour, honor and honour, favor and favour. Other differences include *gray* (American) versus *grey* (British) and *practice* versus *practise*. Unless you think the Britons you're dealing with will be offended, don't worry too much about which variation your documents and correspondence follow, as long as they're consistent.

Schools

In Britain, a *public school* is one that's not part of the state system, and students must pay tuition. (A private school anywhere else, in other words.) If a Briton went to a public school, he or she probably had a middle-class or upper-class upbringing. What Americans would consider a public school would in fact be called a *state school* in Britain.

If a Briton says, "I was at school with him," it means they attended the same grade school and/or high school. For higher education, a Briton would say, "I was at university with him."

Choice Words and Phrases

The British love colorful euphemisms and turns of phrase. "Discussing Ugandan affairs," for example, refers to a man and woman having a clandestine, probably adulterous, affair. Be wary of using phrases about giving or getting "a ride" with someone; to most Irish people and some Britons, this means sexual intercourse. Here are some Briticisms that haven't been previously mentioned, along with their American translations:

- **Afters.** Dessert.
- **Anticlockwise.** Counterclockwise.
- **Back of beyond.** Middle of nowhere.
- **Black Maria.** Paddywagon.
- **Bloody.** Roughly the equivalent of *damned*; particularly offensive if used in reference to a woman.
- **Bobby.** Policeman.
- **Bubble and squeak.** Cabbage and potato.
- **Dear.** Expensive.
- **Fortnight.** Two weeks.
- **Foxed.** Outsmarted.
- **Full stop.** Period (as in punctuation).
- **Git.** A derogatory term for a man; there's no exact translation, but it's very offensive.
- **Gobsmacked.** Amazed, as in open-mouthed amazement.
- **Ground floor.** First floor.
- **Have a go.** Take a turn, try.
- **Intercourse.** A friendly dialogue.
- **In the club.** Pregnant.
- **Jumper.** Sweater.
- **Knackered.** Exhausted.
- **Mate.** Friend.
- **OAP.** Old age pensioner.
- **One stone.** Fourteen pounds.
- **Over the moon.** Elated.

- **Pillock.** Idiot.
- **Quid.** Slang for British pound sterling (money).
- **Row.** Argument.
- **At sixes and sevens.** Overwhelmed, uncertain.
- **Sod off** or **Naff off.** Crude way of telling someone to get lost.
- **The Smoke**. London.
- **Tailback.** Traffic jam.
- **Thick.** Dumb.
- **Thousand million.** Billion.
- **The Tube.** London subway.

Yanks, Limeys & Poms

The British generally don't mind being called *Brits* (they prefer it to "English"), and they see nothing wrong with calling Americans *Yanks*. Ironically, *yankee* was a name originally given by Dutch settlers in New York to British immigrants settling in New England; only later did it come to mean all New Englanders in the colonies, and still later, all Americans to the British. It may have had something to do with "Yankee Doodle Dandy," a tune popular at the time of the American Revolution.

Australians sometimes like to call the British *limeys* or *poms*; the Brits don't appreciate either one. The former refers to the limes that were rationed to British sailors on long sea voyages to prevent scurvy. The latter is short for "pomegranates," a nickname given to English immigrants, whose cheeks flushed a rosy color after their first few days in the unaccustomed Australian sunshine.

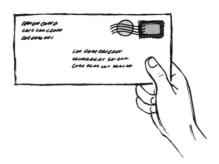

 Correspondence

Mailing (*post*) addresses can be surprisingly tricky. For example:

John Smythe, Esq. (or Mr. John Smythe)
Managing Director
Sugar Plum Productions
The Gingerbread House (many houses and buildings have their own names)
33 Pudding Lane (the actual street address)
Sweet Corner (the neighborhood)
Mirkwood (the district, town or larger neighborhood)
Glasgow GG7 4UU (the city and postal code)
Scotland (the country)

Most addresses are not as long and complicated as the above. The postal code (on the second-to-last line) is so specific that no more than a dozen or two addresses share it, and they're often on the same street. The last line should read England, Scotland, Wales or Northern Ireland, not United Kingdom.

 Useful Numbers

These are local numbers in the U.K. If dialing from outside the U.K., you must use your country's international access code and Britain's country code [44]. And be sure to drop the "0" that precedes the city codes.

Many city codes changed in April 1995. Major ones include: Inner London (0171), Outer London (0181), Birmingham (0121) and Manchester (0161).

- International access code from Britain 001
- International operator 155
- Britain Directory Assistance 192
- Scotland Yard (London police) ..(0171) 230-1212
- British Airways .... (0345) 222-111
- Virgin Atlantic .... (01293) 747-747
- British Rail .... (0171) 387-7070
- London Taxi .... (0171) 286-6010
- British Tourist Authority .... (0181) 846-9000
- American Express .... (0171) 930-4411
- Federal Express (toll free in U.K.) ... (800) 123-800

Books

Living and Working in Britain: A Survival Handbook, by David Hampshire. Surival Books, Surrey, Great Britain, 1991. A detailed resource book with chapters on working conditions, permits and visas, public transport, motoring, shopping and more.

Culture Shock! A Guide to Customs and Etiquette: Britain, by Terry Tan. Graphic Arts Center Publishing Co., Portland, Oregon, USA, 1994. An insightful, witty and often opinionated description of the British.

The Xenophobe's Guide to the English, by Antony Miall. Ravette Books, London, England, 1993. An English public relations executive's review of his country's faults and foibles. Useful, but perhaps a bit too cynical.

The British: Portrait of a People, by Anthony Glyn. G.P. Putnam's Sons, New York, USA, 1970. An affectionate but somewhat dated, treatise on the British character.

The English, by David Frost and Anthony Jay. Stein and Day, New York, USA, 1968. A wickedly funny series of essays by the TV personality David Frost (who began his entertainment career as a joke and skit writer in Britain) and Anthony Jay (scion of an upper-class London family). Their perspective is firmly rooted in the Swinging Sixties, but many of their views still hit the targets today.

Internet Addresses

British Index
> http://www.yacc.co.uk/britind/

BritNet ("The Home of British Commercial Web Sites")
> http://www.britnet.co.uk/

Electronic Yellow Pages, British Telecommunications
> http://www.yell.co.uk/yell/eyp.html

Traveler's World
> http://www.cpoint.co.uk.tw/

U.K. Index
> http://www.ukindex.co.uk/

U.K.-based WWW Servers
> http://src.doc.ic.ac.uk/all-uk.html

Usenet Groups
> clari.world.europe.uk
> soc.culture.uk
> uk.events

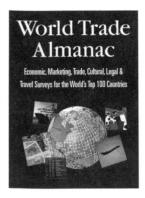